July

by Mari Kesselring
Illustrated by Roberta Collier-Morales

Content Consultant:
Susan Kesselring, MA
Literacy Educator and Preschool Director

magic
wagon

visit us at www.abdopublishing.com

Published by Magic Wagon, a division of the ABDO Group, 8000 West 78th Street, Edina, Minnesota 55439. Copyright © 2010 by Abdo Consulting Group, Inc. International copyrights reserved in all countries. All rights reserved. No part of this book may be reproduced in any form without written permission from the publisher.

Looking Glass Library™ is a trademark and logo of Magic Wagon.

Printed in the United States.

PRINTED ON RECYCLED PAPER

Text by Mari Kesselring
Illustrations by Roberta Collier-Morales
Edited by Holly Saari
Interior layout and design by Emily Love
Cover design by Emily Love

Library of Congress Cataloging-in-Publication Data
Kesselring, Mari.
  July / by Mari Kesselring ; illustrated by Roberta Collier-Morales ; content consultant, Susan Kesselring.
     p. cm. — (Months of the year)
  ISBN 978-1-60270-634-7
  1. July—Juvenile literature. 2. Calendar—Juvenile literature. I. Collier-Morales, Roberta, ill. II. Kesselring, Susan. III. Title.
  CE13.K474 2010
  398'.33—dc22
                          2008050708

Would you like a riddle?

There is one for you here.

Can you name the

seventh month of the year?

Say it out loud.

There's no need to be shy.

You are right!

The seventh month is July!

Grab a ball and a net.

Play volleyball with some friends.

During the summer,
the fun never ends!

July's 31 days fly right by.
Toast marshmallows over a campfire
under a starry sky.

This month's flower
is the water lily.

Wear one as a hat.
You will look silly!

Kaboom! Fireworks light up the night sky. Independence Day is celebrated on the fourth of July.

July gets hot.
Take a trip to the pool!
You can swim with friends
and try to stay cool.

Here's something about July
that you might not guess.
July 19 is Stick Out Your Tongue Day.
It's the best!

July 20 marks
something pretty neat.
The first person made prints
on the moon with his feet!

This month is Hot Dog Month.

Have a bite!

Family and friends

can eat hot dogs all night.

July has been busy.
Now it is done.
Will the month after this
be just as much fun?

23

Moon Walk

Would you like to walk on the moon? Go to a park or a beach and pretend you are walking on moon sand. Make footprints and collect "moon rocks." Then get in your pretend spaceship and blast home!

A Fan for July

It gets pretty hot in July. To stay cool, make your own paper fan. All you need is a piece of paper. Start at one end of the paper and fold over a small section. Then, flip the paper over and fold another small section. Keep folding and flipping until all of the paper is folded. Then, pinch all the folds together at one end of the paper. You are done. Just wave the fan in front of your face!

Words to Know

volleyball—a game with two teams, a large ball, and a high net.
water lily—a flower that grows in bodies of water, such as ponds.

Web Sites

To learn more about July, visit ABDO Group online at **www.abdopublishing.com**. Web sites about July are featured on our Book Links page. These links are routinely monitored and updated to provide the most current information available.